THE
WONDER
WOMAN
WAY

Running Press
Hachette Book Group
1290 Avenue of the Americas, New York, NY 10104
www.runningpress.com
@Running_Press

First Edition: April 2017

Published by Running Press, an imprint of Perseus Books, LLC,
a subsidiary of Hachette Book Group, Inc.

The Hachette Speakers Bureau provides a wide range of
authors for speaking events. To find out more, go to
www.hachettespeakersbureau.com or call (866) 376-6591.

The publisher is not responsible for websites (or their content)
that are not owned by the publisher.

ISBN: 978-0-7624-5694-9

INTRODUCTION

I AM DIANA OF THEMYSCIRA, but that's not the name most know me by. To you in the outside world, in the lands past the shores of my Paradise Island, I am simply called *Wonder Woman*. It's a title I am truly proud of, and a legacy I do my best to uphold every single day of my life.

I grew up a princess on an island untouched by man and the modern ways of society. Raised by my mother, Queen Hippolyta, I was born into royalty, and treated as a daughter of all the Amazon women of mystical Themyscira. It was there I learned the ways of war as well as the art of peace. I was surrounded by natural beauty and some of the best people I have ever encountered. Nevertheless, I was fascinated with the lands beyond our home, and wanted to experience all that the world had to offer.

When a man named *Steve Trevor* crashed his plane on Themyscira, I finally had my chance. My mother called for an emissary to escort Steve back to his home, a mysterious place called the United States of America. To choose this representative of Paradise Island, a grand contest was held. All the Amazons were free to participate, except for one. Worried for my safety, my mother forbade me to enter the games. But my stubbornness rivals hers. I masked my features and joined the contest anyway. And I won.

Despite her reservations, my mother honored her word. I was given a magical costume and lasso and permitted to take *Steve Trevor* back to his homeland. There I became *Wonder Woman*, a Super Hero to those in need, a member of the *Justice League*, and a voice of reason in a reality often devoid of it.

But I'm not alone in my mission to deliver peace to a world locked in chaos. Beside me stand millions of other women and men who share my vision for a better tomorrow. For those already fighting the good fight, I offer this book containing many of my humble life lessons. There is nothing standing between a normal existence and that of a hero. It's just a simple matter of noticing the wonder all around.

LESSON 1

Don't be afraid to make an entrance. Ride in on a big horse, throw the house doors open, and let yourself be known. If you don't have access to a horse, an elephant, bison, or even a magical dragon will do.

However, don't attempt to ride in on anything smaller than a donkey. The person who arrives on the back of a dog is not to be feared and respected, she is to be sat at the children's table and kept away from sharp objects.

LESSON 2

You're going to have fights with your significant other. One of you will forget to do the dishes, or you'll stay out too late, or he'll become mind-controlled by a magical sorceress . . . the thing to remember is, even in the heat of anger, never hit below the belt.

Even if he's Kryptonian.

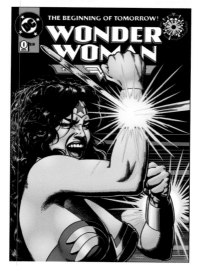

LESSON 3

You're your own worst critic.
Don't beat yourself up.

   Unless one of you happens
to be an evil robotic duplicate.
In that case, go crazy. Knock
yourself out.

LESSON 4

Make sure you listen to your friends. *Really* listen. Even if what they're saying is not what you want to hear.

They're your friends for a reason, and odds are, their advice will be way cheaper than monster divorce court.

LESSON 5

There will be many people in life who criticize you for your clothing choices. They will call you under-dressed, or overdressed, or even poorly dressed, if their sense of style is dramatically different than your own.

Just ignore what they say. Or better yet, throw a tiara at them.

17

LESSON 6

There are those who would have you believe that a woman's place is in the kitchen. Conversely, others will say a woman's place is in the office.

I say that a woman's place is whatever room she happens to walk into.

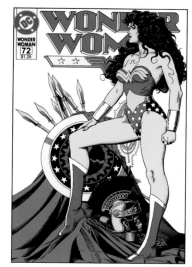

LESSON 7

A battle is like a ballet. Your moves must be lithe yet powerful, striking when needed when the dance directs you to.

To be without grace is to be without wonder.

LESSON 8

People often ask me, "Why *Wonder Woman*?"

I tell them that I simply like the name. I like the word "wonder."

You know, as in, "I wonder when you'll stop talking about this so we can move on to a subject that actually matters in the slightest."

LESSON 9

Some women dress to impress. They wear accessories to emphasize their wardrobe, or to show off their social status.

Personally, I prefer function over fashion. I'll just be over here deflecting bullets.

LESSON 10

You can be anything that you decide to be. Even if the thing you want is to be the president of the United States.

Well, I guess that's not entirely true. I was born on foreign soil, so officially I can't run for the coveted office. Which is probably just as well. After all, someone needs to bail the president out when things get hectic.

LESSON 11

Don't be afraid to reinvent yourself. Not every decision you make will be for the best, and not every chance you take will work out in the long run.

But if you keep to the status quo, you'll never get the chance to wear black leather pants. And if that isn't enough incentive, I don't know what to tell you.

LESSON 12

Pay attention to the little things. Be present in the moment so the details don't pass you by.

Trust me, the last thing you want to do is forget where you parked your Invisible Jet. Seriously, that thing could be anywhere.

LESSON 13

Don't be afraid to take a break once in a while. Remember traditions, relish the holidays. I particularly enjoy the foreign custom of Santa Claus. The tradition allows a person to enter a variety of homes unannounced through the chimney. This can sometimes be helpful in locating a wanted criminal or two.

Plus, I like the red hat.

LESSON 14

There are many sides to everyone. We each have many facets, many volumes under the surface. Sometimes it does a person good to look yourself in the mirror and decide which you is the real one.

And other times, your mirror duplicates will attack you in a fit of rage, but those times are few and far between. So I wouldn't worry too much about it.

LESSON 15

There are people out there who will make you feel like a giant, and constantly put you up on a pedestal. And there are those who will make you feel small, and try to tear you down.

You'll never be smaller than those who attempt to make you feel that way.

LESSON 16

In this life there are those who want you, and those who don't. Don't stress about minds you cannot change, and don't waste your time being pursued by those you don't want in your life.

On a related note, when being hunted, bring a change of clothes. People have a tendency to recognize you easier if you never change out of your Super Hero suit.

LESSON 17 Don't forget where you came from. Your history is an invaluable resource to your future. Only by not repeating the mistakes of your past can you hope to wisely navigate the present.

Of course, this is a little tougher for me than most. The memories of my past have changed so many times, if I didn't know better, I'd think that there's a committee of people constantly altering my life to make it more interesting.

But that would crazy, right?

. . . right?

LESSON 18

Life will try to break you. Life will try to drag through the gutter. It will try to beat you down and crush you.

Other things that will try to crush you? Former apes turned into size-enhanced super-villains named Giganta. Although that may just be something that happens to me, so take that last bit with a grain of salt.

LESSON 19

Go easy on the drama. Life is hard enough as it is without constantly making the demands of a diva. Do everything you can to stay down to earth.

Hint: Being made from clay helps.

LESSON 20

Above all else, make time for fun. On Paradise Island, most won't tell you that life is short. But in the outside world, I've seen its fragility first hand.

So go let your hair down. Smell every flower you pass. Take your Invisible Jet for a joyride.

Tomorrow you may be knee deep in the next big crisis. But today, you're only knee deep in a pair of seriously fierce red boots.

This book has been bound using handcraft methods and Smyth-sewn to ensure durability.

Designed by Ashley Todd.

Cover art adapted by Tom Brannon.

Written by Matthew K. Manning.

Edited by Cindy De La Hoz.

The text was set in Bebas Neue, Benton Sans, and Avenir.